LUCIAN'S TRUE HISTORY

TRANSLATED BY FRANCIS HICKES ILLUS-
TRATED BY WILLIAM STRANG J.B.CLARK
AND AUBREY BEARDSLEY WITH AN IN-
TRODUCTION BY CHARLES WHIBLEY

A. H. BULLEN 18 CECIL COURT
LONDON MCMII

LIST OF ILLUSTRATIONS.

INTRODUCTION.

IT is a commonplace of criticism that Lucian was the first of the moderns, but in truth he is near to our time because of all the ancients he is nearest to his own. With Petronius he shared the discovery that there is material for literature in the debased and various life of every day—that to the seeing eye the individual is more wonderful in colour and complexity than the severely simple abstraction of the poets. He replaced the tradition, respected of his fathers, by an observation more vivid and less pedantic than the note-book of the naturalist. He set the world in the dry light of truth, and since the vanity of mankind is a constant factor throughout the ages, there is scarce a page of Lucian's writing that wears the faded air of antiquity. His personages are as familiar to-day as they were in the second century, because, with his pitiless determination to unravel the tangled skein of human folly, he never blinded his vision to their true qualities. And the multiplicity of his interest is as fresh as his penetration. Nothing came amiss to his eager curiosity. For the first time in the history of literature (with the doubtful exception of Cicero) we encounter a writer whose ceaseless activity includes the world. While others had declared themselves poets, historians, philosophers, Lucian comes forth as a man of letters. Had he lived to-day, he would have edited a newspaper, written leading articles, and kept his name ever before the public in the magazines. For he possessed the qualities, if he avoided the defects, of the journalist. His phrase had not been worn by constant use to imbecility; his sentences were not marred by the association of commonness; his style was still his own and fit for the expression of a personal view. But he noted such types and incidents as make an immediate, if perennial, appeal, and to study him is to be convinced that literature and journalism are not necessarily divorced.

The profession was new, and with the joy of the innovator Lucian was never tired of inventing new *genres*. Romance, criticism, satire—he mastered them all. In *Toxaris* and *The Ass* he proves with what delicacy and restraint he could handle the story. His ill-omened apprenticeship to a sculptor gave him that taste and feeling for art which he turned to so admirable an account. He was, in fact, the first of the art-critics, and he pursued the craft with an easy unconsciousness of the heritage he bequeathed to the world. True, he is silent concerning the technical practice of the Greeks;

true, he leaves us in profound ignorance of the
art of Zeuxis, whose secrets he might have
revealed, had he been less a man of letters.
But he found in painting and sculpture an
opportunity for elegance of phrase, and we
would forgive a thousand shortcomings for such
inspirations of beauty as the smile of Sosandra:
τὸ μειδίαμα σεμνὸν καὶ λεληθός. In literary criticism
he was on surer ground, and here also he
leaves the past behind. His knowledge of
Greek poetry was profound; Homer he had
by heart; and on every page he proves his
sympathies by covert allusion or precise quota-
tion. His treatise concerning the Writing of
History* preserves its force irresistible after
seventeen centuries, nor has the wisdom of the
ages impeached or modified this lucid argument.
With a modest wit he compares himself to
Diogenes, who, when he saw his fellow-citizens
busied with the preparations of war, gathered

* Πῶς δεῖ ἱστορίαν συγγράφειν.

his skirts about him and fell to rolling his tub
up and down. So Lucian, unambitious of
writing history, sheltered himself from "the
waves and the smoke," and was content to
provide others with the best of good counsel.
Yet such is the irony of accident that, as
Lucian's criticism has outlived the masterpieces
of Zeuxis, so the historians have snatched
an immortality from his censure; and let it
be remembered for his glory that he used
Thucydides as a scourge wherewith to beat
impostors. But matters of so high import did
not always engross his humour, and in *The
Illiterate Book-buyer* he satirizes a fashion of
the hour and of all time with a courage and
brutality which tear the heart out of truth.
How intimately does he realize his victim!
And how familiar is this same victim in his
modern shape! You know the very streets
he haunts; you know the very shops wherein

* Πρὸς τὸν ἀπαιδευτὸν καὶ πὸλλα βιβλία ὠνούμενον.

he is wont to acquire his foolish treasures;
you recognize that not by a single trait
has Lucian dishonoured his model. In yet
another strange instance Lucian anticipated
the journalist of to-day. Though his disciples
know it not, he invented the interview. In
that famous visit to the Elysian Fields, which
is a purple patch upon his masterpiece, *The
True History*, he "went to talk with Homer
the Poet, our leisure serving us both well,"
and he put precisely those questions which
the modern hack, note-book in hand, would
seek to resolve. First, remembering the seven
cities, he would know of Homer what father-
land claimed him, and when the poet "said
indeed he was a Babylonian, and among his
own countrymen not called Homer but Tigranes," Lucian straightly "questioned him about
those verses in his books that are disallowed as
not of his making;" whereto Homer replied
with a proper condemnation of Zenodotus and

Aristarchus. And you wonder whether Lucian
is chastising his contemporaries or looking
with the eye of a prophet into the future.

But even more remarkable than his many-
coloured interest is Lucian's understanding.
He was, so to say, a perfect Intelligence thrown
by accident into an age of superstition and cre-
dulity. It is not only that he knew all things :
he saw all things in their right relation. If
the Pagan world had never before been conscious of itself, it had no excuse to harbour
illusions after his coming. Mr. Pater speaks
of the intellectual light he turned upon dim
places, and truly no corner of life escaped the
gleam of his lantern. Gods, philosophers,
necromancers, yielded up their secrets to his
enquiry. With pitiless logic he criticized
their extravagance and pretension ; and actively
anticipating the spirit of modern science, he
accepted no fact, he subscribed to no theory,
which he had not examined with a cold impar-

tiality. Indeed, he was Scepticism in human
shape, but as the weapon of his destruction is
always raillery, as he never takes either himself
or his victims with exaggerated seriousness,
you may delight in his attack, even though
you care not which side wins the battle. His
wit was as mordant as Heine's own;—is it
fantastical to suggest that Lucian too carried
Hebrew blood in his veins?—yet when
the onslaught is most unsparing he is still
joyous. For a gay contempt, not a bitter hatred,
is the note of his satire. And for the very
reason that his scepticism was felt, that it
sprang from a close intimacy with the follies
of his own time, so it is fresh and familiar
to an age that knows not Zeus. Not even the
Dialogues of the Gods are out of date, for if
we no longer reverence Olympus, we still blink
our eyes at the flash of ridicule. And
might not the *Philopseudes*, that masterly
analysis of ghostly terrors, might not

Alexander the False Prophet, have been written yesterday?

And thus we arrive at Lucian's weakness. In spite of its brilliance and flippancy, his scepticism is at times over-intelligent. His good sense baffles you by its infallibility; his sanity is so magnificently beyond question, that you pray for an interlude of unreason. The sprightliness of his wit, the alertness of his fancy, mitigate the perpetual rightness of his judgment. But it must be confessed that for all his delicate sense of ridicule he cherished a misguided admiration of the truth. If only he had understood the joy of self-deception, if only he had realized more often (as he realized in *The Ass*) the delight of throwing probability to the winds, we had regarded him with a more constant affection. His capital defect sprang from a lack of the full-blooded humour which should at times have led him into error. And yet by an irony

b

it was this very love of truth which suggested *The True History*, that enduring masterpiece of phantasy. Setting out to prove his hatred of other men's lies, he shows himself on the road the greatest liar of them all. " The father and founder of all this foolery was Homer's Ulysses": thus he writes in his Preface, confessing that in a spirit of emulation he "turned his style to publish untruths," but with an honester mind, "for this one thing I confidently pronounce for a truth, that I lie." Such is the spirit of the work, nor is there the smallest doubt that Lucian, once embarked upon his voyage, slipped from his ideal, to enjoy the lying for its own sake. If *The True History* fails as a parody, that is because we care not a jot for Ctesias, Iambulus and the rest, at whom the satire is levelled. Its fascination, in fact, is due to those same qualities which, in others, its author affected to despise. The facile variety of its invention can scarce be matched in literature, and the lies are told with so delightful an unconcern, that belief is never difficult. Nor does the narrative ever flag. It ends at the same high level of falsehood in which it has its beginning. And the credibility is increased by the harmonious consistency of each separate lie. At the outset the traveller discovers a river of wine, and forthwith travels up stream to find the source, and "when we were come to the head" (to quote Hickes's translation), "no spring at all appeared, but mighty vine trees of infinite number, which from their roots distilled pure wine, which made the river run so abundantly." So conclusive is the explanation, that you only would have wondered had the stream been of water. And how admirable is the added touch that he who ate fish from the river was made drunk! Then by a pleasant gradation you are carried on from the Hippogypians, or the

Riders of Vultures, every feather in whose wing is bigger and longer than the mast of a tall ship, from the fleas as big as twelve elephants, to those spiders, of mighty bigness, every one of which exceeded in size an isle of the Cyclades. " These were appointed to spin a web in the air between the Moon and the Morning Star, which was done in an instant, and made a plain champaign, upon which the foot forces were planted." Truly a very Colossus of falsehood, but Lucian's ingenuity is inexhausted and inexhaustible, and the mighty Whale is his masterpiece of impudence. For he " contained in greatness fifteen hundred furlongs"; his teeth were taller than beech-trees, and when he swallowed the travellers, he showed himself so far superior to Jonah's fish, that ship and all sailed down his throat, and happily he caught not the pigmy shallop between his chops. And the geographical divisions of the Whale's belly, and

Lucian's adventures therein, are they not set
down with circumstantial verity? Then there
is the episode of the frozen ship, and the sea of
milk, with its well-pressed cheese for an island,
which reminds one of the Elizabethan madri-
gal : "If there were O an Hellespont of Cream."
Moreover, the verisimilitude is enhanced by
a scrupulously simple style. No sooner is
the preface concerning lying at an end than
Lucian lapses into pure narrative. A wealth
of minutely considered detail gives an air of
reality to the most monstrous impossibility;
the smallest facts are explicitly divulged;
the remote accessories described with order
and impressiveness ; so that the wildest invention appears plausible, even inevitable, and you
know that you are in company with the very
genius of falsehood. Nor does this wild diver-
sity of invention suggest romance. It is still
classic in style and shape ; not a phrase nor a
word is lost ; and expression, as always in the

classics, is reduced to its lowest terms. But when the travellers reach the Islands of the Blessed, the style takes on a colour and a beauty which it knew not before. A fragrant air breathed upon them, as of " roses, daffodils, gillyflowers, lilies, violets, myrtles, bays, and blossoms of vines." Happy also was the Isle to look upon : ἔνθα δὴ καὶ καθεωρῶμεν λιμένας τε πολλοὺς περὶ πᾶσαν ἀκλύστους καὶ μεγάλους, ποταμούς τε διαυγεῖς ἐξίοντας ἠρέμα ἐς τὴν θάλατταν· ἔτι δὲ λειμῶνας καὶ ὕλας καὶ ὄρνεα μουσικά, τὰ μὲν ἐπὶ τῶν ἠϊόνων ᾄδοντα, πολλὰ δὲ καὶ ἐπὶ τῶν κλάδων· ἀήρ τε κοῦφος καὶ εὔπνους περιεκέχυτο τὴν χώραν: "a still and gentle air compassing the whole country." Where will you find a more vivid impression of elegance and serenity ? or where match "the melody of the branches, like the sound of wind instruments in a solitary place" (ἀπὸ τῶν κλάδων κινουμένων τερπνὰ καὶ συνεχῆ μέλη ἀπεσυρίζετο ἐοικότα τοῖς ἐπ' ἐρημίας αὐλήμασι τῶν πλαγίων αὐλῶν)? And when the splendour of the city breaks

upon you, with its smaragdus, its cinnamon-
tree, its amethyst, ivory, and beryl, the
rich barbarity suggests Solomon's Temple, or
the City of the Revelation. Its inhabitants
are the occasion of infinite jesting, and again
and again does Lucian satirize the philosophers, his dearest foes. Socrates was in danger
of being thrust forth by Rhadamanthus, ἢν
φλυαρῇ καὶ μὴ ἐθέλῃ ἀφεὶς τὴν εἰρωνείαν εὐωχεῖσθαι,
while as for Diogenes the Sinopean, so pro-
foundly was he changed from his old estate,
that he had married Lais the Harlot. The
journey to Hell is another excuse to gird at
the historians. The severest torments were
inflicted, says Lucian, upon Ctesias the Cnidian, Herodotus and many others, which the
writer beholding "was put in great hopes that
I should never have anything to do there, for I
do not know that ever I spake any untruth in
my life." And yet with all his irony, all his
scorn, Lucian has ever a side-glance at litera-

ture. The verse of Homer is constantly upon his lips, and it is from Homer that the Gods take their ditties in the Elysian fields. Again, when the traveller visits the city of Nephelococcygia, it is but to think upon the poet Aristophanes, "how wise a man he was, and how true a reporter, and how little cause there is to question his fidelity for what he hath written."

Such is the work which, itself a masterpiece, has been a pattern and an exemplar unto others. If Utopia and its unnumbered rivals derive from Plato, there is not a single Imaginary Traveller that is not modelled upon Lucian. *The True History* was, in effect, the beginning of a new literature. Not only was its framework borrowed, not only was its habit of fantastic names piously imitated, but the disciples, like the master, turned their voyages to the purpose of satire. It was Rabelais who made the first adaptation, for, while Epistemon's descent into Hell was certainly suggested by Lucian, Pantagruel's voyage is an ample travesty of *The True History*, and Lanternland, the home of the Lychnobii, is but Lychnopolis, Lucian's own City of Lights. The seventeenth century discovered another imitator in Cyrano de Bergerac, whose tepid *Voyage dans la Lune* is interesting merely because it is a link in the chain that unites Lucian with Swift. Yet the book had an immense popularity, and Cyrano's biographer has naught to say of the original traveller, save that he told his story "avec beaucoup moins de vraisemblance et de gentilesse d'imagination que M. de Bergerac." An astounding judgment surely, which time has already reversed. And then came *Gulliver's Travels*, incomparably the greatest descendant of *The True History*. To what excellent purpose Swift followed his Lucian is proved alike by the amazing probability of his narrative,

and the cruelty of his satire. Like Lucian, he
professed an unveiled contempt for philosophers and mathematicians ; unlike Lucian, he
made his imaginary journey the occasion for a
fierce satire upon kings and politicians. But
so masterly is the narrative, so convincing the
reality of Lilliput and Brobdignag, that *Gulliver* retains its hold upon our imagination,
though the meaning of its satire is long since
blunted. Swift's work came to astonish the
world in 1727, and some fourteen years later
in the century Holberg astonished the wits of
Denmark with a satire cast in Lucian's mould.
Nicolai Klimii Iter Subterraneum—thus ran
the title, and from Latin the book was translated into every known tongue. The city of
walking trees, the home of the Potuans, and
many another invention, prove Holberg's debt
to the author of *The True History*. And if
the *genre* is dead to-day, it is dead because
the most intrepid humourist would hesitate

to walk in the footsteps of Lemuel Gulliver.

Fortunate in his imitators, Lucian has been
not wholly unfortunate in his translators. Not
even envy could pick a quarrel with Francis
Hickes, whose Englishing of *The True History*
is here reprinted. The book appeared, under
the auspices of Hickes's son, in 1634, four
years after the translator's death. Thus it is
described on the title-page : " Certaine Select
Dialogues of Lucian together with his True
Historie, translated from the Greeke into
English by Mr. Francis Hickes. Whereunto
is added the Life of Lucian gathered out of
his own Writings, with briefe Notes and Illus-
trations upon each Dialogue and Booke, by
T. H. Master of Arts, of Christ Church in
Oxford. Oxford, Printed by William Turner.
1634." Composed with a certain dignity, it
is dedicated " to the Right Worshipfull Dr.
Duppa, Deane of Christ-Church, and Vice-

Chancellor of the famous Universitie in Oxford." And the work reflects a wholesome glory upon the famous University. For it is the work of a scholar, who knew both the languages. Though his diction lacked the spirit and colour which distinguished the splendid versions of North and Holland, he was far more keenly conscious of his original than were those masters of prose. Not only did he, unlike North, translate directly from the Greek, but he followed his original with loyalty and patience. In brief, his Lucian is a miracle of suitability. The close simplicity of Hickes fits the classical restraint of *The True History* to admiration. As the Greek is a model of narrative, so you cannot read the English version without thinking of the incomparable Hakluyt. Thirty years after the first printing of the translation, Jasper Mayne published his " Part of Lucian made English," wherein he added sundry versions of his own to the work already

accomplished by Francis Hickes. And in his
"Epistle Dedicatory" he discusses the art of
translation with an intelligence which proves
how intimately he realized the excellent
quality of Hickes's version. "For as the
Painter," thus Jasper Mayne, "who would
draw a man of a bald head, rumpled fore-
head, copper nose, pigge eyes, and ugly face,
draws him not to life, nor doth the business
of his art, if he draw him less deformed or
ugly than he is; or as he who would draw
a faire, amiable lady, limbes with an erring
pencil, and drawes a libell, not a face, if he
gives her not just features, and perfections:
So in the Translation of Bookes, he who
makes a dull author elegant and quick; or
a sharp, elegant author flat, rustick, rude and
dull, by contrary wayes, commits the same
sinne, and cannot be said to translate, but
to transforme." That is sound sense, and
judged by the high standard of Jasper Mayne,

Francis Hickes has most valiantly acquitted himself.

He was the son of Richard Hickes, an arras-weaver of Barcheston, in Warwickshire, and after taking the degree of bachelor in the University of Oxford, which he entered in 1579, at the age of thirteen, he was diverted (says Thomas, his son) " by a country retirement." Henceforth he devoted his life to husbandry and Greek. Besides Lucian, he translated Thucydides and Herodian, the manuscripts of which are said to survive in the library of Christ Church. Possibly it was his long retirement that gave a turn of pedantry to his mind. It was but natural that in his remote garden he should exaggerate the importance of the knowledge acquired in patient solitude. But certain it is that the notes wherewith he decorated his margins are triumphs of inapposite erudition. When Lucian describes the famous cobwebs, each one of which was as big as an island of the Cyclades, Hickes thinks to throw light upon the text with this astonishing irrelevancy: "They are in the Aegean Sea, in number 13." The foible is harmless, nay pleasant, and consonant with the character of the learned recluse. Thus lived Francis Hickes, silent and unknown, until in 1630 he died at a kinsman's house at Sutton in Gloucestershire. And you regret that his glory was merely posthumous. For, pedant as he was, he made known to his countrymen the enemy of all the pedants, and turned a masterpiece of Greek into English as sound and scholarly as is found in any translator of his time.

LUCIAN'S
TRUE HISTORY.

LUCIAN:

HIS TRUE HISTORY.

Even as champions and wrestlers and such as practise the strength and agility of body are not only careful to retain a sound constitution of health, and to hold on their ordinary course of exercise, but sometimes also to recreate themselves with seasonable intermission, and esteem it as a main point of their practice; so I think it necessary for scholars and such as addict themselves to the study of learning, after they have travelled long in the perusal of serious authors, to relax a little the intention of their thoughts, that they may be more apt and able to endure a continued course of study.

And this kind of repose will be the more
conformable, and fit their purpose better, if it
be employed in the reading of such works as
shall not only yield a bare content by the
pleasing and comely composure of them, but
shall also give occasion of some learned specula-
tion to the mind, which I suppose I have
effected in these books of mine : wherein not
only the novelty of the subject, nor the pleasing-
ness of the project, may tickle the reader with
delight, nor to hear so many notorious lies
delivered persuasively and in the way of truth,
but because everything here by me set down
doth in a comical fashion glance at some or
other of the old poets, historiographers, and
philosophers, which in their writings have
recorded many monstrous and intolerable
untruths, whose names I would have quoted

down, but that I knew the reading would
bewray them to you.

Ctesias, the son of Ctesiochus, the Cnidian,
wrote of the region of the Indians and the
state of those countries, matters which he
neither saw himself, nor ever heard come from
the mouth of any man. Iambulus also wrote
many strange miracles of the great sea, which
all men knew to be lies and fictions, yet so
composed that they want not their delight:
and many others have made choice of the
like argument, of which some have published
their own travels and peregrinations, wherein
they have described the greatness of beasts,
the fierce condition of men, with their strange
and uncouth manner of life: but the first
father and founder of all this foolery was
Homer's Ulysses, who tells a long tale to

Alcinöus of the servitude of the winds, and of wild men with one eye in their foreheads that fed upon raw flesh, of beasts with many heads, and the transformation of his friends by enchanted potions, all which he made the silly Phæakes believe for great sooth.

This coming to my perusal, I could not condemn ordinary men for lying, when I saw it in request amongst them that would be counted philosophical persons : yet could not but wonder at them, that, writing so manifest lies, they should not think to be taken with the manner ; and this made me also ambitious to leave some monument of myself behind me, that I might not be the only man exempted from this liberty of lying : and because I had no matter of verity to employ my pen in (for nothing hath befallen me worth the writing),

I turned my style to publish untruths, but
with an honester mind than others have done:
for this one thing I confidently pronounce for
a truth, that I lie: and this, I hope, may be
an excuse for all the rest, when I confess
what I am faulty in: for I write of matters
which I neither saw nor suffered, nor heard
by report from others, which are in no being,
nor possible ever to have a beginning. Let
no man therefore in any case give any credit
to them.

Disanchoring on a time from the pillars
of Hercules, the wind fitting me well for my
purpose, I thrust into the West Ocean. The
occasion that moved me to take such a voyage
in hand was only a curiosity of mind, a desire
of novelties, and a longing to learn out the
bounds of the ocean, and what people inhabit

the farther shore : for which purpose I made
plentiful provision of victuals and fresh water,
got fifty companions of the same humour to
associate me in my travels, furnished myself
with store of munition, gave a round sum of
money to an expert pilot that could direct us
in our course, and new rigged and repaired
a tall ship strongly to hold a tedious and
difficult journey.

Thus sailed we forward a day and a night
with a prosperous wind, and as long as we
had any sight of land, made no great haste
on our way; but the next morrow about sun
rising the wind blew high and the waves
began to swell and a darkness fell upon us,
so that we could not see to strike our sails,
but gave our ship over to the wind and
weather; thus were we tossed in this tempest

the space of threescore and nineteen days
together. On the fourscorth day the sun upon
a sudden brake out, and we descried not far
off us an island full of mountains and woods,
about the which the seas did not rage so
boisterously, for the storm was now reasonably
well calmed : there we thrust in and went on
shore and cast ourselves upon the ground, and
so lay a long time, as utterly tired with our
misery at sea : in the end we arose up and
divided ourselves : thirty we left to guard our
ship : myself and twenty more went to discover
the island, and had not gone above three
furlongs from the sea through a wood, but
we saw a brazen pillar erected, whereupon
Greek letters were engraven, though now much
worn and hard to be discerned, importing,
" Thus far travelled Hercules and Bacchus."

There were also near unto the place two
portraitures cut out in a rock, the one of the
quantity of an acre of ground, the other less,
which made me imagine the lesser to be
Bacchus and the other Hercules : and giving
them due adoration, we proceeded on our
journey, and far we had not gone but we came
to a river, the stream whereof seemed to run
with as rich wine as any is made in Chios,
and of a great breadth, in some places able to
bear a ship, which made me to give the more
credit to the inscription upon the pillar, when
I saw such apparent signs of Bacchus's pere-
grination. We then resolved to travel up
the stream to find whence the river had his
original, and when we were come to the
head, no spring at all appeared, but mighty
great vine-trees of infinite number, which

from their roots distilled pure wine which
made the river run so abundantly: the stream
was also well stored with fish, of which we
took a few, in taste and colour much resembling wine, but as many as ate of them
fell drunk upon it; for when they were opened
and cut up, we found them to be full of lees:
afterwards we mixed some fresh water fish
with them, which allayed the strong taste of
the wine. We then crossed the stream where
we found it passable, and came among a world
of vines of incredible number, which towards
the earth had firm stocks and of a good
growth; but the tops of them were women,
from the hip upwards, having all their proportion perfect and complete; as painters picture
out Daphne, who was turned into a tree when
she was overtaken by Apollo; at their fingers'

ends sprung out branches full of grapes, and the hair of their heads was nothing else but winding wires and leaves, and clusters of grapes. When we were come to them, they saluted us and joined hands with us, and spake unto us some in the Lydian and some in the Indian language, but most of them in Greek : they also kissed us with their mouths, but he that was so kissed fell drunk, and was not his own man a good. while after : they could not abide to have any fruit pulled from them, but would roar and cry out pitifully if any man offered it. Some of them desired to have carnal mixture with us, and two of our company were so bold as to entertain their offer, and could never afterwards be loosed from them, but were knit fast together at their nether parts, from whence they grew

together and took root together, and their
fingers began to spring out with branches
and crooked wires as if they were ready to
bring out fruit: whereupon we forsook them
and fled to our ships, and told the company at
our coming what had betide unto us, how our
fellows were entangled, and of their copulation
with the vines. Then we took certain of our
vessels and filled them, some with water and
some with wine out of the river, and lodged
for that night near the shore.

On the morrow we put to sea again, the
wind serving us weakly, but about noon, when
we had lost sight of the island, upon a sudden
a whirlwind caught us, which turned our ship
round about, and lifted us up some three
thousand furlongs into the air, and suffered
us not to settle again into the sea, but we

hung above ground, and were carried aloft with a mighty wind which filled our sails strongly. Thus for seven days' space and so many nights were we driven along in that manner, and on the eighth day we came in view of a great country in the air, like to a shining island, of a round proportion, gloriously glittering with light, and approaching to it, we there arrived, and took land, and surveying the country, we found it to be both inhabited and husbanded : and as long as the day lasted we could see nothing there, but when night was come many other islands appeared unto us, some greater and some less, all of the colour of fire, and another kind of earth underneath, in which were cities and seas and rivers and woods and mountains, which we conjectured to be the earth by us inhabited : and going

further into the land, we were met withal and
taken by those kind of people which they call
Hippogypians. These Hippogypians are men
riding upon monstrous vultures, which they
use instead of horses : for the vultures there
are exceeding great, every one with three
heads apiece : you may imagine their greatness
by this, for every feather in their wings was
bigger and longer than the mast of a tall ship :
their charge was to fly about the country, and
all the strangers they found to bring them to
the king : and their fortune was then to seize
upon us, and by them we were presented to
him. As soon as he saw us, he conjectured by
our habit what countrymen we were, and said,
Are not you, strangers, Grecians ? which when
we affirmed, And how could you make way,
said he, through so much air as to get hither ?

Then we delivered the whole discourse of our
fortunes to him ; whereupon he began to tell
us likewise of his own adventures, how that
he also was a man, by name Endymion, and
rapt up long since from the earth as he was
asleep, and brought hither, where he was
made king of the country, and said it was
that region which to us below seemed to be
the moon ; but he bade us be of good cheer
and fear no danger, for we should want nothing
we stood in need of : and if the war he was
now in hand withal against the sun succeeded
fortunately, we should live with him in the
highest degree of happiness. Then we asked
of him what enemies he had, and the cause of
the quarrel : and he answered, Phaethon, the
king of the inhabitants of the sun (for that
is also peopled as well as the moon), hath made

war against us a long time upon this occasion :
I once assembled all the poor people and needy
persons within my dominions, purposing to
send a colony to inhabit the Morning Star,
because the country was desert and had nobody
dwelling in it. This Phaethon envying, crossed
me in my design, and sent his Hippomyrmicks
to meet with us in the midway, by whom we
were surprised at that time, being not prepared
for an encounter, and were forced to retire :
now therefore my purpose is once again to
denounce war and publish a plantation of
people there : if therefore you will participate
with us in our expedition, I will furnish you
every one with a prime vulture and all
armour answerable for service, for to-morrow
we must set forwards. With all our hearts,
said I, if it please you. Then were we feasted

c

and abode with him, and in the morning
arose to set ourselves in order of battle, for
our scouts had given us knowledge that the
enemy was at hand. Our forces in number
amounted to an hundred thousand, besides
such as bare burthens and engineers, and the
foot forces and the strange aids: of these,
fourscore thousand were Hippogypians, and
twenty thousand that rode upon Lachanopters,
which is a mighty great fowl, and instead of
feathers covered thick over with wort leaves;
but their wing feathers were much like the
leaves of lettuces: after them were placed the
Cenchrobolians and the Scorodomachians:
there came also to aid us from the Bear Star
thirty thousand Psyllotoxotans, and fifty
thousand Anemodromians: these Psyllotoxotans ride upon great fleas, of which they have

their denomination, for every flea among them
is as big as a dozen elephants: the Anemodromians are footmen, yet flew in the air
without feathers in this manner: every man
had a large mantle reaching down to his foot,
which the wind blowing against, filled it like
a sail, and they were carried along as if they
had been boats: the most part of these in
fight were targeteers. It was said also that
there were expected from the stars over
Cappadocia threescore and ten thousand
Struthobalanians and five thousand Hippo-
geranians, but I had no sight of them, for
they were not yet come, and therefore I
durst write nothing, though wonderful and
incredible reports were given out of them.
This was the number of Endymion's army;
the furniture was all alike; their helmets of

bean hulls, which are great with them and
very strong; their breastplates all of lupins
cut into scales, for they take the shells of
lupins, and fastening them together, make
breastplates of them which are impenetrable
and as hard as any horn: their shields and
swords like to ours in Greece: and when the
time of battle was come, they were ordered in
this manner. The right wing was supplied by
the Hippogypians, where the king himself was
in person with the choicest soldiers in the
army, among whom we also were ranged: the
Lachanopters made the left wing, and the
aids were placed in the main battle as every
man's fortune fell: the foot, which in number
were about six thousand myriads, were disposed of in this manner: there are many
spiders in those parts of mighty bigness,

every one in quantity exceeding one of the Islands Cyclades : these were appointed to spin a web in the air between the Moon and the Morning Star, which was done in an instant, and made a plain champaign upon which the foot forces were planted, who had for their leader Nycterion, the son of Eudianax, and two other associates.

But of the enemy's side the left wing consisted of the Hippomyrmicks, and among them Phaethon himself : these are beasts of huge bigness and winged, carrying the resemblance of our emmets, but for their greatness : for those of the largest size were of the quantity of two acres, and not only the riders supplied the place of soldiers, but they also did much mischief with their horns : they were in number fifty thousand. In the right wing were ranged

the Aeroconopes, of which there were also
about fifty thousand, all archers riding upon
great gnats : then followed the Aerocardakes,
who were light armed and footmen, but good
soldiers, casting out of slings afar off huge
great turnips, and whosoever was hit with
them lived not long after, but died with the
stink that proceeded from their wounds : it is
said they use to anoint their bullets with
the poison of mallows. After them were
placed the Caulomycetes, men-at-arms and
good at hand strokes, in number about
fifty thousand : they are called Caulomycetes
because their shields were made of mushrooms and their spears of the stalks of the
herb asparagus : near unto them were placed
the Cynobalanians, that were sent from the
Dogstar to aid him : these were men with

dogs' faces, riding upon winged acorns : but
the slingers that should have come out of
Via Lactea, and the Nephelocentaurs came too
short of these aids, for the battle was done
before their arrival, so that they did them no
good : and indeed the slingers came not at
all, wherefore they say Phaethon in displeasure
over-ran their country. These were the forces
that Phaethon brought into the field : and
when they were joined in battle, after the
signal was given, and when the asses on
either side had brayed (for these are to them
instead of trumpets), the fight began, and
the left wing of the Heliotans, or Sun soldiers,
fled presently and would not abide to receive
the charge of the Hippogypians, but turned
their backs immediately, and many were put
to the sword : but the right wing of theirs

were too hard for our left wing, and drove
them back till they came to our footmen, who
joining with them, made the enemies there
also turn their backs and fly, especially when
they found their own left wing to be over-
thrown. Thus were they wholly discomfited
on all hands; many were taken prisoners,
and many slain; much blood was spilt; some
fell upon the clouds, which made them look
of a red colour, as sometimes they appear to
us about sun-setting; some dropped down
upon the earth, which made me suppose it
was upon some such occasion that Homer
thought Jupiter rained blood for the death of
his son Sarpedon. Returning from the pur-
suit, we erected two trophies: one for the
fight on foot, which we placed upon the
spiders' web: the other for the fight in the

air, which we set up upon the clouds. As soon as this was done, news came to us by our scouts that the Nephelocentaurs were coming on, which indeed should have come to Phaethon before the fight. And when they drew so near unto us that we could take full view of them, it was a strange sight to behold such monsters, composed of flying horses and men : that part which resembled mankind, which was from the waist upwards, did equal in greatness the Rhodian Colossus, and that which was like a horse was as big as a great ship of burden : and of such multitude that I was fearful to set down their number lest it might be taken for a lie : and for their leader they had the Sagittarius out of the Zodiac. When they heard that their friends were foiled, they sent a messenger to Phaethon

to renew the fight: whereupon they set themselves in array, and fell upon the Selenitans or
the Moon soldiers that were troubled, and
disordered in following the chase, and scattered
in gathering the spoils, and put them all to
flight, and pursued the king into his city, and
killed the greatest part of his birds, overturned
the trophies he had set up, and overcame the
whole country that was spun by the spiders.
Myself and two of my companions were taken
alive. When Phaethon himself was come they
set up other trophies in token of victory, and
on the morrow we were carried prisoners into
the Sun, our arms bound behind us with a
piece of the cobweb: yet would they by no
means lay any siege to the city, but returned
and built up a wall in the midst of the air
to keep the light of the Sun from falling upon

the Moon, and they made it a double wall,
wholly compact of clouds, so that a manifest
eclipse of the Moon ensued, and all things
detained in perpetual night : wherewith
Endymion was so much oppressed that he
sent ambassadors to entreat the demolishing
of the building, and beseech him that he
would not damn them to live in darkness,
promising to pay him tribute, to be his friend
and associate, and never after to stir against
him. Phaethon's council twice assembled to
consider upon this offer, and in their first
meeting would remit nothing of their conceived
displeasure, but on the morrow they altered
their minds to these terms. " The Heliotans
and their colleagues have made a peace with
the Selenitans and their associates upon these
conditions, that the Heliotans shall cast down

the wall, and deliver the prisoners that they
have taken upon a ratable ransom : and that
the Selenitans should leave the other stars
at liberty, and raise no war against the
Heliotans, but aid and assist one another if
either of them should be invaded : that the
king of the Selenitans should yearly pay to
the king of the Heliotans in way of tribute ten
thousand vessels of dew, and deliver ten
thousand of their people to be pledges for
their fidelity : that the colony to be sent to
the Morning Star should be jointly supplied
by them both, and liberty given to any else
that would to be sharers in it : that these
articles of peace should be engraven in a
pillar of amber, to be erected in the midst
of the air upon the confines of their country :
for the performance whereof were sworn of

the Heliotans, Pyronides and Therites and
Phlogius: and of the Selenitans, Nyctor and
Menius and Polylampes." Thus was the peace
concluded, the wall immediately demolished,
and we that were prisoners delivered. Being
returned into the Moon, they came forth
to meet us, Endymion himself and all his
friends, who embraced us with tears, and
desired us to make our abode with him, and
to be partners in the colony, promising to
give me his own son in marriage (for there are
no women amongst them), which I by no
means would yield unto, but desired of all
loves to be dismissed again into the sea,
and he finding it impossible to persuade us
to his purpose, after seven days' feasting,
gave us leave to depart.

Now, what strange novelties worthy of

note I observed during the time of my abode
there, I will relate unto you. The first is, that
they are not begotten of women, but of mankind : for they have no other marriage but
of males : the name of women is utterly
unknown among them : until they accom-
plish the age of five and twenty years, they
are given in marriage to others : from that
time forwards they take others in marriage
to themselves : for as soon as the infant is
conceived the leg begins to swell, and afterwards when the time of birth is come, they
give it a lance and take it out dead : then they
lay it abroad with open mouth towards the
wind, and so it takes life : and I think thereof
the Grecians call it the belly of the leg, because
therein they bear their children instead of
a belly. I will tell you now of a thing more

strange than this There are a kind of men among them called Dendritans, which are begotten in this manner: they cut out the right stone out of a man's cod, and set it in their ground, from which springeth up a great tree of flesh, with branches and leaves, bearing a kind of fruit much like to an acorn, but of a cubit in length, which they gather when they are ripe, and cut men out of them: their privy members are to be set on and taken off as they have occasion: rich men have them made of ivory, poor men of wood, wherewith they perform the act of generation and accompany their spouses.

When a man is come to his full age he dieth not, but is dissolved like smoke and is turned into air. One kind of food is common to them all, for they kindle a fire and broil frogs upon the

coals, which are with them in infinite numbers
flying in the air, and whilst they are broiling,
they sit round about them as it were about a
table, and lap up the smoke that riseth from
them, and feast themselves therewith, and
this is all their feeding. For their drink they
have air beaten in a mortar, which yieldeth
a kind of moisture much like unto dew. They
have no avoidance of excrements, either of
urine or dung, neither have they any issue
for that purpose like unto us. Their boys
admit copulation, not like unto ours, but
in their hams, a little above the calf of
the leg, for there they are open. They hold
it a great ornament to be bald, for hairy
persons are abhorred with them, and yet
among the stars that are comets it is thought
commendable, as some that have travelled

those coasts reported unto us. Such beards
as they have are growing a little above their
knees. They have no nails on their feet, for
their whole foot is all but one toe. Every
one of them at the point of his rump hath a
long colewort growing out instead of a tail,
always green and flourishing, which though
a man fall upon his back, cannot be broken.
The dropping of their noses is more sweet than
honey. When they labour or exercise themselves, they anoint their body with milk,
whereinto if a little of that honey chance to
drop, it will be turned into cheese. They
make very fat oil of their beans, and of as
delicate a savour as any sweet ointment. They
have many vines in those parts, which yield
them but water : for the grapes that hang upon
the clusters are like our hailstones : and I verily

think that when the vines there are shaken
with a strong wind, there falls a storm of hail
amongst us by the breaking down of those
kind of berries. Their bellies stand them
instead of satchels to put in their necessaries,
which they may open and shut at their
pleasure, for they have neither liver nor any
kind of entrails, only they are rough and hairy
within, so that when their young children are
cold, they may be enclosed therein to keep
them warm. The rich men have garments
of glass, very soft and delicate: the poorer
sort of brass woven, whereof they have great
plenty, which they enseam with water to make
it fit for the workman, as we do our wool. If
I should write what manner of eyes they have,
I doubt I should be taken for a liar in publish-
ing a matter so incredible : yet I cannot choose

but tell it : for they have eyes to take in and out as please themselves : and when a man is so disposed, he may take them out and lay them by till he have occasion to use them, and then put them in and see again : many when they have lost their own eyes, borrow of others, for the rich have many lying by them. Their ears are all made of the leaves of plane-trees, excepting those that come of acorns, for they only have them made of wood.

I saw also another strange thing in the same court : a mighty great glass lying upon the top of a pit of no great depth, whereinto, if any man descend, he shall hear everything that is spoken upon the earth : if he but look into the glass, he shall see all cities and all nations as well as if he were among them. There had I the sight of all my friends and the whole country about : whether they saw me or not I cannot tell : but if they believe it not to be so, let them take the pains to go thither themselves and they shall find my words true. Then we took our leaves of the king and such as were near him, and took shipping and departed : at which time Endymion bestowed upon me two mantles made of their glass, and five of brass, with a complete armour of those shells of lupins, all which I left behind me in the whale : and sent with us a thousand of his Hippogypians to conduct us five hundred furlongs on our way. In our course we coasted many other countries, and lastly arrived at the Morning Star now newly inhabited, where we landed and took in fresh water : from thence we entered the Zodiac, passing by the Sun, and, leaving it on our right hand, took our course near unto the shore, but landed not in the country, though our company did much desire it, for the wind would not give us leave: but we saw it was a flourishing region, fat and well watered, abounding with all delights : but the Nephelo-centaurs espying us, who were mercenary soldiers to Phaethon, made to our ship as fast as they could, and finding us to be friends, said no more unto us, for our Hippogypians were departed before. Then we made for-wards all the next night and day, and about evening-tide following we came to a city called Lychnopolis, still holding on our course down-wards. This city is seated in the air between the Pleiades and the Hyades, somewhat lower than the Zodiac, and arriving there, not a man was to be seen, but lights in great numbers

running to and fro, which were employed, some
in the market place, and some about the haven,
of which many were little, and as a man may
say, but poor things ; some again were great
and mighty, exceeding glorious and resplen-
dent, and there were places of receipt for them
all ; every one had his name as well as men ;
and we did hear them speak. These did us
no harm, but invited us to feast with them,
yet we were so fearful, that we durst neither
eat nor sleep as long as we were there. Their
court of justice standeth in the midst of the
city, where the governor sitteth all the night
long calling every one by name, and he that
answereth not is adjudged to die, as if he had
forsaken his ranks. Their death is to be
quenched. We also standing amongst them
saw what was done, and heard what answers

the lights made for themselves, and the reasons they alleged for tarrying so long : there we also knew our own light, and spake unto it, and questioned it of our affairs at home, and how all did there, which related everything unto us. That night we made our abode there, and on the next morrow returned to our ship, and sailing near unto the clouds had a sight of the city Nephelococcygia, which we beheld with great wonder, but entered not into it, for the wind was against us. The king thereof was Coronus, the son of Cottyphion : and I could not choose but think upon the poet Aristophanes, how wise a man he was, and how true a reporter, and how little cause there is to question his fidelity for what he hath written.

The third after, the ocean appeared plainly

unto us, though we could see no land but
what was in the air, and those countries also
seemed to be fiery and of a glittering colour.
The fourth day about noon, the wind gently
forbearing, settled us fair and leisurely into the
sea; and as soon as we found ourselves upon
water, we were surprised with incredible glad-
ness, and our joy was unexpressible; we
feasted and made merry with such provision
as we had; we cast ourselves into the sea,
and swam up and down for our disport, for
it was a calm. But oftentimes it falleth out
that the change to the better is the beginning
of greater evils: for when we had made only
two days' sail in the water, as soon as the
third day appeared, about sun-rising, upon a
sudden we saw many monstrous fishes and
whales: but one above the rest, containing in

greatness fifteen hundred furlongs, which came gaping upon us and troubled the sea round about him, so that he was compassed on every side with froth and foam, showing his teeth afar off, which were longer than any beech trees are with us, all as sharp as needles, and as white as ivory: then we took, as we thought, our last leaves one of another, and embracing together, expected our ending day. The monster was presently with us, and swallowed us up ship and all; but by chance he caught us not between his chops, for the ship slipped through the void passages down into his entrails. When we were thus got within him we continued a good while in darkness, and could see nothing till he began to gape, and then we perceived it to be a monstrous whale of a huge breadth and height, big enough to contain a city that would hold ten thousand men : and within we found small fishes and many other creatures chopped in pieces, and the masts of ships and anchors and bones of men and luggage. In the midst of him was earth and hills, which were raised, as I conjectured, by the settling of the mud which came down his throat, for woods grew upon them and trees of all sorts and all manner of herbs, and it looked as if it had been husbanded. The compass of the land was two hundred and forty furlongs : there were also to be seen all kind of sea fowl, as gulls, halcyons and others that had made their nests upon the trees. Then we fell to weeping abundantly, but at the last I roused up my company, and propped up our ship and struck fire. Then we made ready supper of such as we had,

for abundance of all sort of fish lay ready by us, and we had yet water enough left which we brought out of the Morning Star. The next morrow we rose to watch when the whale should gape : and then looking out, we could sometimes see mountains, sometimes only the skies, and many times islands, for we found that the fish carried himself with great swiftness to every part of the sea. When we grew weary of this, I took seven of my company, and went into the wood to see what I could find there, and we had not gone above five furlongs but we light upon a temple erected to Neptune, as by the title appeared, and not far off we espied many sepulchres and pillars placed upon them, with a fountain of clear water close unto it : we also heard the barking of a dog, and saw smoke rise afar off, so that we judged there was some dwelling thereabout. Wherefore making the more haste, we lighted upon an old man and a youth, who were very busy in making a garden and in conveying water by a channel from the fountain into it : whereupon we were surprised both with joy and fear : and they also were brought into the same taking, and for a long time remained mute. But after some pause, the old man said, What are ye, you strangers? any of the sea spirits? or miserable men like unto us? for we that are men by nature, born and bred in the earth, are now sea-dwellers, and swim up and down within the Continent of this whale, and know not certainly what to think of ourselves : we are like to men that be dead, and yet believe ourselves to be alive. Whereunto I answered, For our parts, father, we are

men also, newly come hither, and swallowed
up ship and all but yesterday : and now come
purposely within this wood which is so large
and thick : some good angel, I think, did
guide us hither to have the sight of you,
and to make us know that we are not the
only men confined within this monster : tell
us therefore your fortunes, we beseech you,
what you are, and how you came into this
place. But he answered, You shall not hear
a word from me, nor ask any more questions
until you have taken part of such viands as
we are able to afford you. So he took us
and brought us into his house, which was
sufficient to serve his turn : his pallets were
prepared, and all things else made ready.
Then he set before us herbs and nuts and
fish, and filled out of his own wine unto us :

and when we were sufficiently satisfied, he
then demanded of us what fortunes we had
endured, and I related all things to him in
order that had betide unto us, the tempest,
the passages in the island, our navigation in
the air, our war, and all the rest, even till
our diving into the whale. Whereat he
wondered exceedingly, and began to deliver
also what had befallen to him, and said, By
lineage, O ye strangers, I am of the isle
Cyprus, and travelling from mine own country
as a merchant, with this my son you see here,
and many other friends with me, made a
voyage for Italy in a great ship full fraught
with merchandise, which perhaps you have
seen broken in pieces in the mouth of the
whale. We sailed with fair weather till we
were as far as Sicily, but there we were over-

taken with such a boisterous storm that the third day we were driven into the ocean, where it was our fortune to meet with this whale which swallowed us all up, and only we two escaped with our lives; all the rest perished, whom we have here buried and built a temple to Neptune. Ever since we have continued this course of life, planting herbs and feeding upon fish and nuts : here is wood enough, you see, and plenty of vines which yield most delicate wine : we have also a well of excellent cool water, which it may be you have seen : we make our beds of the leaves of trees, and burn as much wood as we will : we chase after the birds that fly about us, and go out upon the gills of the monster to catch after live fishes : here we bathe ourselves when we are disposed, for we have a lake of salt water not far off,

about some twenty furlongs in compass, full of
sundry sorts of fish, in which we swim and
sail upon it in a little boat of mine own
making. This is the seven-and-twentieth year
of our drowning, and with all this we might be
well enough contented if our neighbours and
borderers about us were not perverse and
troublesome, altogether insociable and of stern
condition. Is it so, indeed, said I, that there
should be any within the whale but your-
selves? Many, said he, and such as are un-
reconcilable towards strangers, and of monstrous and deformed proportions. The western
countries and the tail-part of the wood are
inhabited by the Tarychanians that look like
eels, with faces like a lobster: these are warlike, fierce, and feed upon raw flesh: they
that dwell towards the right side are called

Tritonomendetans, which have their upper parts like unto men, their lower parts like cats, and are less offensive than the rest. On the left side inhabit the Carcinochirians and the Thinnocephalians, which are in league one with another : the middle region is possessed by the Paguridians, and the Psettopodians, a warlike nation and swift of foot : eastwards towards the mouth is for the most part desert, as over-washed by the sea : yet am I fain to take that for my dwelling, paying yearly to the Psetto-podians in way of tribute five hundred oysters.

Of so many nations doth this country consist. We must therefore devise among ourselves either how to be able to fight with them, or how to live among them. What number may they all amount unto? said I. More than a thousand, said he. And what armour have

E

they? None at all, said he, but the bones
of fishes. Then were it our best course, said I,
to encounter them, being provided as we are,
and they without weapons, for if we prove too
hard for them we shall afterward live out of
fear. This we concluded upon, and went to
our ship to furnish ourselves with arms. The
occasion of war we gave by non-payment of
tribute, which then was due, for they sent their
messengers to demand it, to whom he gave a
harsh and scornful answer, and sent them
packing with their arrant. But the Psetto-
podians and Paguridians, taking it ill at the
hands of Scintharus, for so was the man named,
came against us with great tumult: and we,
suspecting what they would do, stood upon our
guard to wait for them, and laid five-and-
twenty of our men in ambush, commanding

them as soon as the enemy was passed by to set upon them, who did so, and arose out of their ambush, and fell upon the rear. We also being five-and-twenty in number (for Scintharus and his son were marshalled among us) advanced to meet with them, and encountered them with great courage and strength : but in the end we put them to flight and pursued them to their very dens. Of the enemies were slain an hundred threescore and ten, and but one of us besides Trigles, our pilot, who was thrust through the back with a fish's rib. All that day following and the night after we lodged in our trenches, and set on end a dry backbone of a dolphin instead of a trophy.

The next morrow the rest of the country people, perceiving what had happened, came to

assault us.   The Tarychanians were ranged in
the right wing, with Pelamus their captain : the
Thinnocephalians were placed in the left wing :
the Carcinochirians made up the main battle :
for the Tritonomendetans stirred not, neither
would they join with either part.   About the
temple of Neptune we met with them, and
joined fight with a great cry, which was
answered with an echo out of the whale as if
it had been out of a cave : but we soon put
them to flight, being naked people, and chased
them into the wood, making ourselves masters
of the country.   Soon after they sent ambassadors to us to crave the bodies of the dead
and to treat upon conditions of peace ; but we
had no purpose to hold friendship with them,
but set upon them the next day and put them
all to the sword except the Tritonomendetans,

who, seeing how it fared with the rest of their
fellows, fled away through the gills of the fish,
and cast themselves into the sea. Then we
travelled all the country over, which now was
desert, and dwelt there afterwards without fear
of enemies, spending the time in exercise of the
body and in hunting, in planting vineyards and
gathering fruit of the trees, like such men as
live delicately and have the world at will, in a
spacious and unavoidable prison. This kind
of life led we for a year and eight months, but
when the fifth day of the ninth month was
come, about the time of the second opening of
his mouth (for so the whale did once every
hour, whereby we conjectured how the hours
went away), I say about the second opening,
upon a sudden we heard a great cry and a
mighty noise like the calls of mariners and the

stirring of oars, which troubled us not a little.
Wherefore we crept up to the very mouth of
the fish, and standing within his teeth, saw
the strangest sight that ever eye beheld—men
of monstrous greatness, half a furlong in
stature, sailing upon mighty great islands as if
they were upon shipboard. I know you will
think this smells like a lie, but yet you shall
have it. The islands were of a good length
indeed, but not very high, containing about an
hundred furlongs in compass; every one of
these carried of those kind of men eight-and-
twenty, of which some sat on either side of the
island and rowed in their course with great
cypress trees, branches, leaves and all, instead
of oars. On the stern or hinder part, as I take
it, stood the governor, upon a high hill, with a
brazen rudder of a furlong in length in his

hand : on the fore-part stood forty such fellows as those, armed for the fight, resembling men in all points but in their hair, which was all fire and burnt clearly, so that they needed no helmets. Instead of sails the wood growing in the island did serve their turns, for the wind blowing against it drave forward the island like a ship, and carried it which way the governor would have it, for they had pilots to direct them, and were as nimble to be stirred with oars as any long-boat. At the first we had the sight but of two or three of them : afterwards appeared no less than six hundred, which, dividing themselves in two parts, prepared for encounter, in which many of them by meeting with their barks together were broken in pieces, many were turned over and drowned : they that closed, fought lustily and would not easily be parted, for the soldiers in the front showed a great deal of valour, entering one upon another, and killed all they could, for none were taken prisoners. Instead of iron grapples they had mighty great polypodes fast tied, which they cast at the other, and if they once laid hold on the wood they made the isle sure enough for stirring. They darted and wounded one another with oysters that would fill a wain, and sponges as big as an acre. The leader on the one side was Æolocentaurus, and of the other Thalassopotes. The quarrel, as it seems, grew about taking a booty: for they said that Thalassopotes drave away many flocks of dolphins that belonged to Æolocentaurus, as we heard by their clamours one to another, and calling upon the names of their kings: but Æolocentaurus had the better of

the day and sunk one hundred and fifty of the
enemy's islands, and three they took with the
men and all. The rest withdrew themselves
and fled, whom the other pursued, but not
far, because it grew towards evening, but returned to those that were wrecked and broken,
which they also recovered for the most part,
and took their own away with them : for on
their part there were no less than fourscore
islands drowned. Then they erected a trophy
for a monument of this island fight, and
fastened one of the enemy's islands with a
stake upon the head of the whale. That night
they lodged close by the beast, casting their
cables about him, and anchored near unto him :
their anchors are huge and great, made of
glass, but of a wonderful strength. The
morrow after, when they had sacrificed upon

the top of the whale, and there buried their dead, they sailed away, with great triumph and songs of victory. And this was the manner of the islands' fight.

LUCIAN:

HIS TRUE HISTORY.

THE SECOND BOOK.

Upon this we began to be weary of our
abode in the whale, and our tarriance there did
much trouble us. We therefore set all our
wits a-work to find out some means or other to
clear us from our captivity. First, we thought
it would do well to dig a hole through his
right side and make our escape that way forth,
which we began to labour at lustily ; but after
we had pierced him five furlongs deep and
found it was to no purpose, we gave it over.
Then we devised to set the wood on fire, for

that would certainly kill him without all question, and being once dead, our issue would be
easy enough. This we also put in practice,
and began our project at the tail end, which
burnt seven days and as many nights before he
had any feeling of our fireworks: upon the
eighth and ninth days we perceived he began
to grow sickly: for he gaped more dully than
he was wont to do, and sooner closed his
mouth again: the tenth and eleventh he was
thoroughly mortified and began to stink: upon
the twelfth day we bethought ourselves, though
almost too late, that unless we underpropped
his chops when he gaped next to keep them
from closing, we should be in danger of perpetual imprisonment within his dead carcase
and there miserably perish. We therefore
pitched long beams of timber upright within

his mouth to keep it from shutting, and then
made our ship in a readiness, and provided
ourselves with store of fresh water, and all
other things necessary for our use, Scintharus
taking upon him to be our pilot, and the next
morrow the whale died.   Then we hauled our
ship through the void passages, and fastening
cables about his teeth, by little and little settled
it into the sea, and mounting the back of the
whale, sacrificed to Neptune, and for three
days together took up our lodging hard by the
trophy, for we were becalmed.   The fourth day
we put to sea, and met with many dead corpses
that perished in the late sea-fight, which our
ship hit against, whose bodies we took measure
of with great admiration, and sailed for a few
days in very temperate weather.   But after that
the north wind blew so bitterly that a great

frost ensued, wherewith the whole sea was all
frozen up, not only superficially upon the upper
part, but in depth also the depth of four
hundred fathoms, so that we were fain to for-
sake our ship and run upon the ice. The
wind sitting long in this corner, and we not
able to endure it, put this device in practice,
which was the invention of Scintharus :—with
mattocks and other instruments we made a
mighty cave in the water, wherein we sheltered
ourselves forty days together : in it we kindled
fire, and fed upon fish, of which we found great
plenty in our digging. At the last, our provision falling short, we returned to our frozen
ship, which we set upright, and spreading her
sails, went forward as well as if we had been
upon water, leisurely and gently sliding upon
the ice; but on the fifth day the weather grew

warm, and the frost brake, and all was turned
to water again. We had not sailed three
hundred furlongs forwards but we came to a
little island that was desert, where we only
took in fresh water (which now began to fail
us), and with our shot killed two wild bulls,
and so departed. These bulls have their horns
growing not upon their heads but under their
eyes, as Momus thought it better. Then we
entered into a sea, not of water but of milk, in
which appeared a white island full of vines.
This island was only a great cheese well
pressed (as we afterwards found when we fed
upon it), about some five-and-twenty furlongs
in bigness: the vines were full of clusters of
grapes, out of which we could crush no wine,
but only milk: in the midst of the island there
was a temple built dedicated to Galatea, one

of the daughters of Nereus, as by the inscription appeared. As long as we remained there the soil yielded us food and victuals, and our drink was the milk that came out of the grapes : in these, as they said, reigneth Tyro, the daughter of Salmoneus, who, after her departure, received this guerdon at the hands of Neptune.

In this island we rested ourselves five days, and on the sixth put to sea again, a gentle gale attending us, and the seas all still and quiet. The eighth day, as we sailed onward, not in milk any longer, but in salt and azure water, we saw many men running upon the sea, like unto us every way forth, both in shape and stature, but only for their feet, which were of cork, whereupon, I suppose, they had the name of Phellopodes.

We marvelled much when we saw they did not sink, but keep above water, and travel upon it so boldly. These came unto us, and saluted us in the Grecian language, and said they were bound towards Phello, their own country, and for a while ran along by us, but at last turned their own way and left us, wishing us a happy and prosperous voyage. Within a while after many islands appeared, and near unto them, upon our left hand, stood Phello, the place whereunto they were travelling, which was a city seated upon a mighty great and round cork. Further off, and more towards the right hand, we saw five other islands, large and mountainous, in which much fire was burning; but directly before us was a spacious flat island, distant from us not above five hundred fur-longs: and approaching somewhat near unto it,

F

a wonderful fragrant air breathed upon us, of a most sweet and delicate smell, such as Herodotus, the story-writer, saith ariseth out of Arabia the happy, consisting of a mixture of roses, daffodils, gillyflowers, lilies, violets, myrtles, bays, and blossoms of vines: such a dainty odoriferous savour was conveyed unto us.

Being delighted with this smell, and hoping for better fortunes after our long labours, we got within a little of the isle, in which we found many havens on every side, not subject to overflowing, and yet of great capacity, and rivers of clear water emptying themselves easily into the sea, with meadows and herbs and musical birds, some singing upon the shore, and many upon the branches of trees, a still and gentle air compassing the whole country. When pleasant blasts gently stirred the woods the motion of the branches made a continual delightsome melody, like the sound of wind instruments in a solitary place : a kind of clamour also was heard mixed with it, yet not tumultuous nor offensive, but like the noise of a banquet, when some do play on wind instruments, some commend the music, and some with their hands applaud the pipe, or the harp. All which yielded us so great content that we boldly entered the haven, made fast our ship and landed, leaving in her only Scintharus and two more of our companions behind us. Passing along through a sweet meadow we met with the guards that used to sail about the island, who took us and bound us with garlands of roses (which are the strictest bands they have), to be carried to their governor :

from them we heard, as we were upon the way,
that it was the island of those that are called
blessed, and that Rhadamanthus was governor
there, to whom we were brought and placed the
fourth in order of them that were to be
judged.

The first trial was about Ajax, the son of
Telamon, whether he were a meet man to be
admitted into the society of the Heroes or
not : the objections against him were his mad-
ness and the killing of himself : and after long
pleading to and fro, Rhadamanthus gave this
sentence, that for the present he should be
put to Hippocrates, the physician of Cos, to
be purged with helleborus, and upon the
recovery of his wits to have admittance.

The second was a controversy of love, Theseus and Menelaus contending which had the

better right to Helen ; but Rhadamanthus gave
judgment on Menelaus' side, in respect of the
manifold labours and perils he had incurred
for that marriage' sake, whereas Theseus had
wives enough beside to live withal—as the
Amazon, and the daughters of Minos. The
third was a question of precedency between
Alexander, the son of Philip, and Hannibal,
the Carthaginian, in which Alexander was preferred, and his throne placed next to the elder
Cyrus the Persian.

In the fourth place we appeared, and
he demanded of us what reason we had,
being living men, to take land in that sacred
country, and we told him all our adventures
in order as they befell us : then he com-
manded us to stand aside, and considering
upon it a great while, in the end proposed it

to the benchers, which were many, and among them Aristides the Athenian, surnamed the Just : and when he was provided what sentence to deliver, he said that for our busy curiosity and needless travels we should be accountable after our death ; but for the present we should have a time limited for our abode, during which we should feast with the Heroes and then depart, prefixing us seven months' liberty to conclude our tarriance, and no more. Then our garlands fell off from us of themselves, and we were set loose and led into the city to feast with the blessed.

The city was all of gold, compassed with a wall made of the precious stone smaragdus, which had seven gates, every one cut out of a whole piece of timber of cinnamon-tree : the pavement of the city

and all the ground within the walls was
ivory: the temples of all the gods are built of
beryl, with large altars made all of one whole
amethyst, upon which they offer their sacri-
fices: about the city runneth a river of most
excellent sweet ointment, in breadth an hundred cubits of the larger measure, and so deep
that a man may swim in it with ease. For
their baths they have great houses of glass,
which they warm with cinnamon: and their
bathing-tubs are filled with warm dew instead
of water. Their only garments are cobwebs
of purple colour; neither have they any bodies,
but are intactile and without flesh, a mere
shape and presentation only: and being thus
bodiless, they yet stand, and are moved, are
intelligent, and can speak: and their naked
soul seemeth to wander up and down in a

corporal likeness: for if a man touch them not
he cannot say otherwise, but that they have
bodies, altogether like shadows standing upright, and not, as they are, of a dark colour.
No man waxeth any older there than he was
before, but of what age he comes thither, so
he continues. Neither is there any night with
them, nor indeed clear day: but like the
twilight towards morning before the sun be
up, such a kind of light do they live in. They
know but one season of the year which is the
spring, and feel no other wind but Zephyrus.
The region flourisheth with all sorts of flowers,
and with all pleasing plants fit for shade: their
vines bear fruit twelve times a year, every
month once: their pomegranate-trees, their
apple-trees, and their other fruit, they say,
bear thirteen times in the year, for in the

month called Minous they bear twice. Instead of wheat their ears bear them loaves
of bread ready baked, like unto mushrooms.
About the city are three hundred three-score
and five wells of water, and as many of
honey, and five hundred of sweet ointment,
for they are less than the other. They
have seven rivers of milk and eight of
wine.

They keep their feast without the city
in a field called Elysium, which is a most
pleasant meadow, environed with woods of
all sorts, so thick that they serve for a
shade to all that are invited, who sit upon
beds of flowers, and are waited upon, and
have everything brought unto them by the
winds, unless it be to have the wine filled:
and that there is no need of: for about the

banqueting place are mighty great trees growing of clear and pure glass, and the fruit of
those trees are drinking-cups and other kind
of vessels of what fashion or greatness you
will: and every man that comes to the feast
gathers one or two of those cups, and sets
them before him, which will be full of wine
presently, and then they drink. Instead of
garlands the nightingales and other musical
birds gather flowers with their beaks out of
the meadows adjoining, and flying over their
heads with chirping notes scatter them among
them.

They are anointed with sweet ointment
in this manner: sundry clouds draw that
unguent out of the fountains and the rivers,
which settling over the heads of them that
are at the banquet, the least blast of wind

makes a small rain fall upon them like unto
a dew. After supper they spend the time in
music and singing: their ditties that are in
most request they take out of Homer's verses,
who is there present himself and feasteth
among them, sitting next above Ulysses: their
choirs consist of boys and virgins, which were
directed and assisted by Eunomus the Locrian, and Arion the Lesbian, and Anacreon,
and Stesichorus, who hath had a place there
ever since his reconcilement with Helena. As
soon as these have done there enter a second
choir of swans, swallows, and nightingales;
and when they have ended, the whole woods
ring like wind-instruments by the stirring of
the air.

But that which maketh most for their
mirth are two wells adjoining to the ban-

queting place, the one of laughter, the
other of pleasure : of these every man drinks
to begin the feast withal, which makes
them spend the whole time in mirth and
laughter.

I will also relate unto you what famous men
I saw in that association. There were all the
demigods, and all that fought against Troy,
excepting Ajax the Locrian : he only, they
told me, was tormented in the region of the
unrighteous. Of barbarians there was the
elder and the younger Cyrus, and Anacharsis
the Scythian, Zamolxis the Thracian, and
Numa the Italian. There was also Lycurgus
the Lacedæmonian, and Phocion and Tellus
the Athenians, and all the Wise Men, unless
it were Periander.

I also saw Socrates, the son of Sophro-

niscus, prattling with Nestor and Palamedes,
and close by him stood Hyacinthus the
Lacedæmonian, and the gallant Narcissus
and Hylas, and other beautiful and lovely
youths, and for aught I could gather by
him he was far in love with Hyacinthus,
for he discoursed with him more than all the
rest : for which cause, they said, Rhadamanthus was offended at him, and often threatened
to thrust him out of the island if he continued
to play the fool in that fashion, and not give
over his idle manner of jesting, when he was
at their banquet. Only Plato was not present,
for they said he dwelled in a city framed by
himself, observing the same rule of govern-
ment and laws as he had prescribed for them
to live under.

Aristippus and Epicurus are prime men

amongst them, because they are the most
jovial good fellows and the best companions.
Diogenes the Sinopean was so far altered
from the man he was before that he married
with Lais the harlot, and was many times
so drunk that he would rise and dance about
the room as a man out of his senses. Æsop
the Phrygian served them for a jester. There
was not one Stoic in company but were still
busied in ascending the height of virtue's
hill: and of Chrysippus we heard that it
was not lawful for him by any means to
touch upon the island until he have the fourth
time purged himself with helleborus. The
Academics, they say, were willing enough to
come, but that they yet are doubtful and in
suspense, and cannot comprehend how there
should be any such island; but indeed, I

think, they were fearful to come to be judged
by Rhadamanthus, because themselves have
abolished all kind of judgment: yet many
of them, they say, had a desire, and would
follow after those that were coming hither,
but were so slothful as to give it over
because they were not comprehensive, and
therefore turned back in the midst of their
way.

These were all the men of note that I saw
there; and amongst them all Achilles was
held to be the best man, and next to him
Theseus. For their manner of venery and
copulation thus it is: they couple openly in
the eyes of all men, both with females and
male kind, and no man holds it for any
dishonesty. Only Socrates would swear
deeply that he accompanied young men in

a cleanly fashion, and therefore every man condemned him for a perjured fellow: and Hyacinthus and Narcissus both confessed otherwise for all his denial.

The women there are all in common, and no man takes exception at it, in which respect they are absolutely the best Platonists in the world: and so do the boys yield themselves to any man's pleasure without contradiction.

After I had spent two or three days in this manner, I went to talk with Homer the poet, our leisure serving us both well, and to know of him what countryman he was, a question with us hard to be resolved, and he said he could not certainly tell himself, because some said he was of Chios, some of Smyrna, and many to be of Colo-

phon; but he said indeed he was a Babylonian, and among his own countrymen not
called Homer but Tigranes, and afterwards
living as an hostage among the Grecians,
he had therefore that name put upon him.
Then I questioned him about those verses
in his books that are disallowed as not of
his making, whether they were written by
him or not, and he told me they were all
his own, much condemning Zenodotus and
Aristarchus, the grammarians, for their weakness in judgment.

When he had satisfied me in this, I asked
him again why he began the first verse of
his poem with anger: and he told me it fell
out so by chance, not upon any premedita-
tion. I also desired to know of him whether
he wrote his Odysseys before his Iliads, as

many men do hold: but he said it was not
so. As for his blindness which is charged
upon him, I soon found it was far otherwise, and perceived it so plainly that I needed
not to question him about it.

Thus was I used to do many days when
I found him idle, and would go to him and
ask him many questions, which he would
give me answer to very freely: especially
when we talked of a trial he had in the court
of justice, wherein he got the better: for
Thersites had preferred a bill of complaint
against him for abusing him and scoffing at
him in his Poem, in which action Homer
was acquitted, having Ulysses for his advo-
cate.

About the same time came to us Pythagoras
the Samian, who had changed his shape now

seven times, and lived in as many lives, and accomplished the periods of his soul. The right half of his body was wholly of gold; and they all agreed that he should have place amongst them, but were doubtful what to call him, Pythagoras or Euphorbus. Empedocles also came to the place, scorched quite over, as if his body had been broiled upon the embers; but could not be admitted for all his great entreaty.

The time passing thus along, the day of prizes for masteries of activity now approached, which they call Thanatusia. The setters of them forth were Achilles the fifth time, and Theseus the seventh time. To relate the whole circumstance would require a long discourse, but the principal points I will deliver. At wrestling Carus, one of the lineage of

G 2

Hercules, had the best, and wan the garland
from Ulysses. The fight with fists was equal
between Arius the Ægyptian, who was buried
at Corinth, and Epius, that combated for it.
There was no prize appointed for the Pancra-
tian fight: neither do I remember who got
the best in running: but for poetry, though
Homer without question were too good for
them all, yet the best was given to Hesiodus.
The prizes were all alike, garlands plotted of
peacocks' feathers.

As soon as the games were ended, news
came to us that the damned crew in the
habitation of the wicked had broken their
bounds, escaped the gaolers, and were coming
to assail the island, led by Phalaris the Agri-
gentine, Busyris the Ægyptian, Diomedes the
Thracian, Sciron, Pituocamptes, and others:

which Rhadamanthus hearing, he ranged the
Heroes in battle array upon the sea-shore,
under the leading of Theseus and Achilles
and Ajax Telamonius, who had now recovered
his senses, where they joined fight ; but the
Heroes had the day, Achilles carrying himself
very nobly. Socrates also, who was placed
in the right wing, was noted for a brave
soldier, much better than he was in his lifetime, in the battle at Delium : for when the
enemy charged him, he neither fled nor
changed countenance : wherefore afterwards,
in reward of his valour, he had a prize set
out for him on purpose, which was a beautiful
and spacious garden, planted in the suburbs
of the city, whereunto he invited many, and
disputed with them there, giving it the name
of Necracademia.

Then we took the vanquished prisoners, and bound them, and sent them back to be punished with greater torments.

This fight was also penned by Homer, who, at my departure, gave me the book to show my friends, which I afterwards lost and many things else beside : but the first verse of the poem I remember was this: " Tell me now, Muse, how the dead Heroes fought." ·

When they overcome in fight, they have a custom to make a feast with sodden beans, wherewith they banquet together for joy of their victory : only Pythagoras had no part with them, but sat aloof off, and lost his dinner because he could not away with beans.

Six months were now passed over, and the seventh halfway onwards, when a new

business was begot amongst us. For Cinyras the son of Scintharus, a proper tall young man, had long been in love with Helena, and it might plainly be perceived that she as fondly doted upon him, for they would still be winking and drinking one to another whilst they were a-feasting, and rise alone together, and wander up and down in the wood. This humour increasing, and knowing not what course to take, Cinyras' device was to steal away Helena, whom he found as pliable to run away with him, to some of the islands adjoining, either to Phello, or Tyroessa, having before combined with three of the boldest fellows in my company to join with them in their conspiracy; but never acquainted his father with it, knowing that he would surely punish him for it.

Being resolved upon this, they watched their time to put it in practice: for when night was come, and I absent (for I was fallen asleep at the feast), they gave a slip to all the rest, and went away with Helena to shipboard as fast as they could. Menelaus waking about midnight, and finding his bed empty, and his wife gone, made an outcry, and calling up his brother, went to the court of Rhadamanthus.

As soon as the day appeared, the scouts told them they had descried a ship, which by that time was got far off into the sea. Then Rhadamanthus set out a vessel made of one whole piece of timber of asphodelus wood, manned with fifty of the Heroes to pursue after them, which were so willing on their way, that by noon they had overtaken them newly entered into the milky ocean, not far from Tyroessa, so near were they got to make an escape. Then took we their ship and hauled it after us with a chain of roses and brought it back again.

Rhadamanthus first examined Cinyras and his companions whether they had any other partners in this plot, and they confessing none, were adjudged to be tied fast by the privy members and sent into the place of the wicked, there to be tormented, after they had been scourged with rods made of mallows. Helena, all blubbered with tears, was so ashamed of herself that she would not show her face. They also decreed to send us packing out of the country, our prefixed time being come, and that we should stay there no longer than the next morrow: where-

with I was much aggrieved and wept bitterly
to leave so good a place and turn wanderer
again I knew not whither: but they com-
forted me much in telling me that before
many years were past I should be with them
again, and showed me a chair and a bed
prepared for me against the time to come
near unto persons of the best quality.

Then went I to Rhadamanthus, humbly
beseeching him to tell me my future fortunes,
and to direct me in my course; and he told
me that after many travels and dangers, I
should at last recover my country, but would
not tell me the certain time of my return:
and showing me the islands adjoining, which
were five in number, and a sixth a little
further off, he said, Those nearest are the
islands of the ungodly, which you see burn-

ing all in a light fire, but the other sixth
is the island of dreams, and beyond that is
the island of Calypso, which you cannot see
from hence. When you are past these, you
shall come into the great continent, over
against your own country, where you shall
suffer many afflictions, and pass through
many nations, and meet with men of inhuman
conditions, and at length attain to the other
continent.

When he had told me this, he plucked a
root of mallows out of the ground, and
reached it to me, commanding me in my
greatest perils to make my prayers to that:
advising me further neither to rake in the
fire with my knife, nor to feed upon lupins,
nor to come near a boy when he is past
eighteen years of age : if I were mindful of

this, the hopes would be great that I should come to the island again.

Then we prepared for our passage, and feasted with them at the usual hour, and next morrow I went to Homer, entreating him to do so much as make an epigram of two verses for me, which he did: and I erected a pillar of berylstone near unto the haven, and engraved them upon it. The epigram was this:

> Lucian, the gods' belov'd, did once attain
> To see all this, and then go home again.

After that day's tarrying, we put to sea, brought onward on our way by the Heroes, where Ulysses closely coming to me that Penelope might not see him, conveyed a

letter into my hand to deliver to Calypso in
the isle of Ogygia. Rhadamanthus also sent
Nauplius, the ferryman, along with us, that
if it were our fortune to put into those
islands, no man should lay hands upon us,
because we were bent upon other employ-
ments.

No sooner had we passed beyond the smell
of that sweet odour but we felt a horrible
filthy stink, like pitch and brimstone burning,
carrying an intolerable scent with it as if men
were broiling upon burning coals: the air
was dark and muddy, from which distilled a
pitchy kind of dew. We heard also the lash
of the whips, and the roarings of the tormented: yet went we not to visit all the
islands, but that wherein we landed was of
this form: it was wholly compassed about

with steep, sharp, and craggy rocks, without either wood or water: yet we made a shift to scramble up among the cliffs, and so went forwards in a way quite overgrown with briars. and thorns through a most villainous ghastly country, and coming at last to the prison and place of torment we wondered to see the nature and quality of the soil, which brought forth no other flowers but swords and daggers, and round about it ran certain rivers, the first of dirt, the second of blood, and the innermost of burning fire, which was very broad and unpassable, floating like water, and working like the waves of the sea, full of sundry fishes, some as big as firebrands, others of a less size like coals of fire, and these they call Lychniscies.

There was but one narrow entrance into it,

and Timon of Athens appointed to keep the
door, yet we got in by the help of Nauplius,
and saw them that were tormented, both
kings and private persons very many, of
which there were some that I knew, for there
I saw Cinyras tied by private members, and
hanging up in the smoke. But the greatest
torments of all are inflicted upon them that
told any lies in their lifetime, and wrote
untruly, as Ctesias the Cnidian, Herodotus,
and many other, which I beholding, was put
in great hopes that I should never have anything to do there, for I do not know that
ever I spake any untruth in my life. We
therefore returned speedily to our ship (for
we could endure the sight no longer), and
taking our leaves of Nauplius, sent him back
again.

A little after appeared the Isle of Dreams
near unto us, an obscure country and un-
perspicuous to the eye, endued with the
same quality as dreams themselves are: for
as we drew, it still gave back and fled
from us, that it seemed to be farther
off than at the first, but in the end we
attained it and entered the haven called
Hypnus, and adjoined to the gate of
ivory, where the temple of Alectryon stands,
and took land somewhat late in the evening.

Entering the gate we saw many dreams of
sundry fashions; but I will first tell you
somewhat of the city, because no man else
hath written any description of it: only
Homer hath touched it a little, but to small
purpose.

It is round about environed with a wood, the trees whereof are exceeding high poppies and mandragoras, in which an infinite number of owls do nestle, and no other birds to be seen in the island: near unto it is a river running, called by them Nyctiporus, and at the gates are two wells, the one named Negretus, the other Pannychia. The wall of the city is high and of a changeable colour, like unto the rainbow, in which are four gates, though Homer speak but of two: for there are two which look toward the fields of sloth, the one made of iron, the other of potter's clay, through which those dreams have passage that represent fearful, bloody, and cruel matters: the other two behold the haven and the sea, of which the one is made of

H

horn, the other of ivory, which we went in at.

As we entered the city, on the right hand stands the temple of the Night, whom, with Alectryon, they reverence above all the gods : for he hath also a temple built for him near unto the haven. On the left hand stands the palace of sleep, for he is the sovereign king over them all, and hath deputed two great princes to govern under him, namely, Taraxion, the son of Matogenes, and Plutocles, the son of Phantasion.

In the middest of the market-place is a well, by them called Careotis, and two temples adjoining, the one of falsehood, the other of truth, which have either of them a private cell peculiar to the priests,

and an oracle, in which the chief prophet is Antiphon, the interpreter of dreams, who was preferred by Sleep to that place of dignity.

These dreams are not all alike either in nature or shape, for some of them are long, beautiful, and pleasing: others again are as short and deformed. Some make show to be of gold, and others to be as base and beggarly. Some of them had wings, and were of monstrous forms: others set out in pomp, as it were in a triumph, representing the appearances of kings, gods, and other persons.

Many of them were of our acquaintance, for they had been seen of us before, which came unto us and saluted us as their old friends, and took us and lulled us asleep,

H 2

and feasted us nobly and courteously, promising beside all other entertainment which
was sumptuous and costly, to make us kings
and princes. Some of them brought us home
to our own country to show us our friends
there, and come back with us the next
morrow.

Thus we spent thirty days and as many
nights among them, sleeping and feasting
all the while, until a sudden clap of thunder
awakened us all, and we starting up, provided ourselves of victuals, and took sea
again, and on the third day landed in
Ogygia. But upon the way I opened the
letter I was to deliver, and read the contents,
which were these:

"Ulysses to Calypso sendeth greeting.
This is to give you to understand that after

my departure from you in the vessel I made
in haste for myself, I suffered shipwreck,
and hardly escaped by the help of Leucothea
into the country of the Phæacks, who sent
me to mine own home, where I found many
that were wooers to my wife, and riotously
consumed my means; but I slew them all,
and was afterwards killed myself by my son
Telegonus, whom I begat of Circe, and am
now in the island of the blessed, where I
daily repent myself for refusing to live with
you, and forsaking the immortality proffered
me by you; but if I can spy a convenient
time, I will give them all the slip and come
to you."

This was the effect of the letter, with
some addition concerning us, that we should
have entertainment: and far had I not gone

from the sea but I found such a cave as
Homer speaks of, and she herself working
busily at her wool. When she had received
the letter, and brought us in, she began to
weep and take on grievously, but afterwards
she called us to meat, and made us very
good cheer, asking us many questions concerning Ulysses and Penelope, whether she
was so beautiful and modest as Ulysses had
often before bragged of her.

And we made her such answer as we
thought would give her best content: and
departing to our ship, reposed ourselves near
unto the shore, and in the morning put to
sea, where we were taken with a violent
storm, which tossed us two days together,
and on the third we fell among the Colocynthopiratans. These are a wild kind of men,

that issue out of the islands adjoining, and prey upon passengers, and for their shipping have mighty great gourds six cubits in length, which they make hollow when they are ripe, and cleanse out all that is within them, and use the rinds for ships, making their masts of reeds, and their sails of the gourd leaves.

These set upon us with two ships furnished and fought with us, and wounded many, casting at us instead of stones the seeds of those gourds. The fight was continued with equal fortune until about noon, at which time, behind the Colocynthopiratans, we espied the Caryonautans coming on, who, as it appeared, were enemies to the other, for when they saw them approach, they forsook us and turned about to fight with

them; and in the mean space we hoist sail
and away, leaving them together by the ears,
and no doubt but the Caryonautans had the
better of the day, for they exceeded in number, having five ships well furnished, and
their vessels of greater strength, for they are
made of nutshells cloven in the midst and
cleansed, of which every half is fifteen fathom
in length.

When we were got out of sight we were
careful for the curing of our hurt men, and
from that time forwards went no more un-
armed, fearing continually to be assaulted on
the sudden: and good cause we had: for
before sunsetting some twenty men or there-
abouts, which also were pirates, made towards
us, riding upon monstrous great dolphins,
which carried them surely: and when their

riders gat upon their backs, would neigh like horses. When they were come near us, they divided themselves, some on the one side, and some on the other, and flung at us with dried cuttle-fishes and the eyes of sea-crabs: but when we shot at them again and hurt them, they would not abide it, but fled to the island, the most of them wounded.

About midnight, the sea being calm, we fell before we were aware upon a mighty great halcyon's nest, in compass no less than threescore furlongs, in which the halcyon herself sailed, as she was hatching her eggs, in quantity almost equalling the nest, for when she took her wings, the blast of her feathers had like to have overturned our ship, making a lamentable noise as she flew along.

As soon as it was day, we got upon it, and found it to be a nest, fashioned like a great lighter, with trees plaited and wound one within another, in which were five hundred eggs, every one bigger than a tun of Chios measure, and so near their time of hatching that the young chickens might be seen and began to cry. Then with an axe we hewed one of the eggs in pieces, and cut out a young one that had no feathers, which yet was bigger than twenty of our vultures.

When we had gone some two hundred furlongs from this nest, fearful prodigies and strange tokens appeared unto us, for the carved goose, that stood for an ornament on the stern of our ship, suddenly flushed out with feathers and began to cry. Scintharus, our pilot, that was a bald man, in an instant was covered with hair: and which was more strange than all the rest, the mast of our ship began to bud out with branches and to bear fruit at the top, both of figs and great clusters of grapes, but not yet ripe. Upon the sight of this we had great cause to be troubled in mind, and therefore besought the gods to avert from us the evil that by these tokens was portended.

And we had not passed full out five hundred furlongs, but we came in view of a mighty wood of pine-trees and cypress, which made us think it had been land, when it was indeed a sea of infinite depth, planted with trees that had no roots, but floated firm and upright, standing upon the water. When we came to it and found how the

case stood with us, we knew not what to do
with ourselves. To go forwards through the
trees was altogether impossible: they were
so thick and grew so close together: and to
turn again with safety was as much unlikely.

I therefore got me up to the top of the
highest tree to discover, if I could, what
was beyond; and I found the breadth of
the wood to be fifty furlongs or thereabout, and then appeared another ocean
to receive us. Wherefore we thought it
best to assay to lift up our ship upon the
leaves of the trees which were thick grown,
and by that means pass over, if it were
possible, to the other ocean: and so we
did: for fastening a strong cable to our
ship, we wound it about the tops of the
trees, and with much ado poised it up to

the height, and placing it upon the branches, spread our sails, and were carried as it were upon the sea, dragging our ship after us by the help of the wind which set it forwards. At which time a verse of the poet Antimachus came to my remembrance, wherein he speaks of sailing over tops of trees.

When we had passed over the wood, and were come to the sea again, we let down our ship in the same manner as we took it up. Then sailed we forwards in a pure and clear stream, until we came to an exceeding great gulf or trench in the sea, made by the division of the waters as many times is upon land, where we see great clefts made in the ground by earthquakes and other means. Whereupon we struck sail

and our ship stayed upon a sudden when
it was at the pit's brim ready to tumble
in : and we stooping down to look into it,
thought it could be no less than a thousand furlongs deep, most fearful and monstrous to behold, for the water stood as it
were divided into two parts, but looking
on our right hand afar off, we perceived a
bridge of water, which to our seeming, did
join the two seas together and crossed over
from the one to the other. Wherefore we
laboured with oars to get unto it, and over
it we went and with much ado got to
the further side beyond all our expectation.

Then a calm sea received us, and in it
we found an island, not very great, but
inhabited with unsociable people, for in it
were dwelling wild men named Bucepha-

lians, that had horns on their heads like
the picture of Minotaurus, where we went
ashore to look for fresh water and victuals,
for ours was all spent : and there we found
water enough, but nothing else appeared;
only we heard a great bellowing and roar-
ing a little way off, which we thought to
have been some herd of cattle, and going
forwards, fell upon those men, who espying
us, chased us back again, and took three of
our company : the rest fled towards the sea.

Then we all armed ourselves, not meaning to leave our friends unrevenged, and
set upon the Bucephalians as they were
dividing the flesh of them that were slain,
and put them all to flight, and pursued
after them, of whom we killed fifty,
and two we took alive, and so returned

with our prisoners; but food we could find none.

Then the company were all earnest with me to kill those whom we had taken; but I did not like so well of that, thinking it better to keep them in bonds until ambassadors should come from the Bucephalians to ransom them that were taken, and indeed they did: and I well understood by the nodding of their heads, and their lamentable lowing, like petitioners, what their business was.

So we agreed upon a ransom of sundry cheeses and dried fish and onions and four deer with three legs apiece, two behind and one before. Upon these conditions we delivered those whom we had taken, and tarrying there but one day, departed.

Then the fishes began to show themselves in the sea, and the birds flew over our heads, and all other tokens of our approach to land appeared unto us. Within a while after we saw men travelling the seas, and a new found manner of navigation, themselves supplying the office both for ship and sailor, and I will tell you how. As they lie upon their backs in the water and their privy members standing upright, which are of a large size and fit for such a purpose, they fasten thereto a sail, and holding their cords in their hands, when the wind hath taken it, are carried up and down as please themselves.

After these followed others riding upon cork, for they yoke two dolphins together, and drive them on (performing themselves the place of a coachman), which draw the cork along after them. These never offered us

I

any violence, nor once shunned our sight ; but
passed along in our company without fear, in a
peaceable manner, wondering at the greatness
of our ship, and beholding it on every side.

At evening we arrived upon a small island,
inhabited, as it seemed, only by women,
which could speak the Greek language ; for
they came unto us, gave us their hands,
and saluted us, all attired like wantons,
beautiful and young, wearing long mantles
down to the foot: the island was called
Cabbalusa and the city Hydramardia. So
the women received us, and every one of
them took aside one of us for herself, and
made him her guest. But I pausing a
little upon it (for my heart misgave me),
looked narrowly round about, and saw the
bones of many men, and the skulls lying

together in a corner; yet I thought not good to make any stir, or to call my company about me, or to put on arms; but taking the mallow into my hand, made my earnest prayers thereto that I might escape out of those present perils.

Within a while after, when the strange female came to wait upon me, I perceived she had not the legs of a woman, but the hoofs of an ass. Whereupon I drew my sword, and taking fast hold of her, bound her, and examined her upon the point: and she, though unwillingly, confessed that they were sea-women, called Onosceleans, and they fed upon strangers that travelled that way. For, said she, when we have made them drunk, we go to bed to them, and in their sleep, make a hand of them.

I hearing this, left her bound in the

place where she was, and went up to the roof of the house, where I made an outcry, and called my company to me, and when they were come together, acquainted them with all that I had heard, and showed them the bones, and brought them into her that was bound, who suddenly was turned into water, and could not be seen. Notwithstanding, I thrust my sword into the water to see what would come of it, and it was changed into blood.

Then we made all the haste we could to our ship, and got us away, and as soon as it was clear day, we had sight of the mainland, which we judged to be the country opposite to our continent. Whereupon we worshipped, and made our prayers, and took council what was now to be done. Some thought it best only to go a-land and so return back again: others

thought it better to leave our ship there and march into the mid-land to try what the inhabitants would do: but whilst we were upon this consultation a violent storm fell upon us, which drave our ship against the shore, and burst it all in pieces, and with much ado we all swam to land with our arms, every man catching what he could lay hands on.

These are all the occurrences I can acquaint you withal, till the time of our landing, both in the sea, and in our course to the islands, and in the air, and after that in the whale; and when we came out again what betid unto us among the Heroes and among the dreams, and lastly among the Bucephalians and the Onosceleans. What passed upon land the next books shall deliver.

Ingram Content Group UK Ltd.
Milton Keynes UK
UKHW022326050623
422929UK00005B/336

9 781015 695443